P9-CRC-421

28287

SUNSET ELEMENTARY
MEDIA CENTER

DIVE!

MY ADVENTURES IN THE DEEP FRONTIER

SUNSET ELEMENTARY
MEDIA CENTER

Dive!

My Adventures In

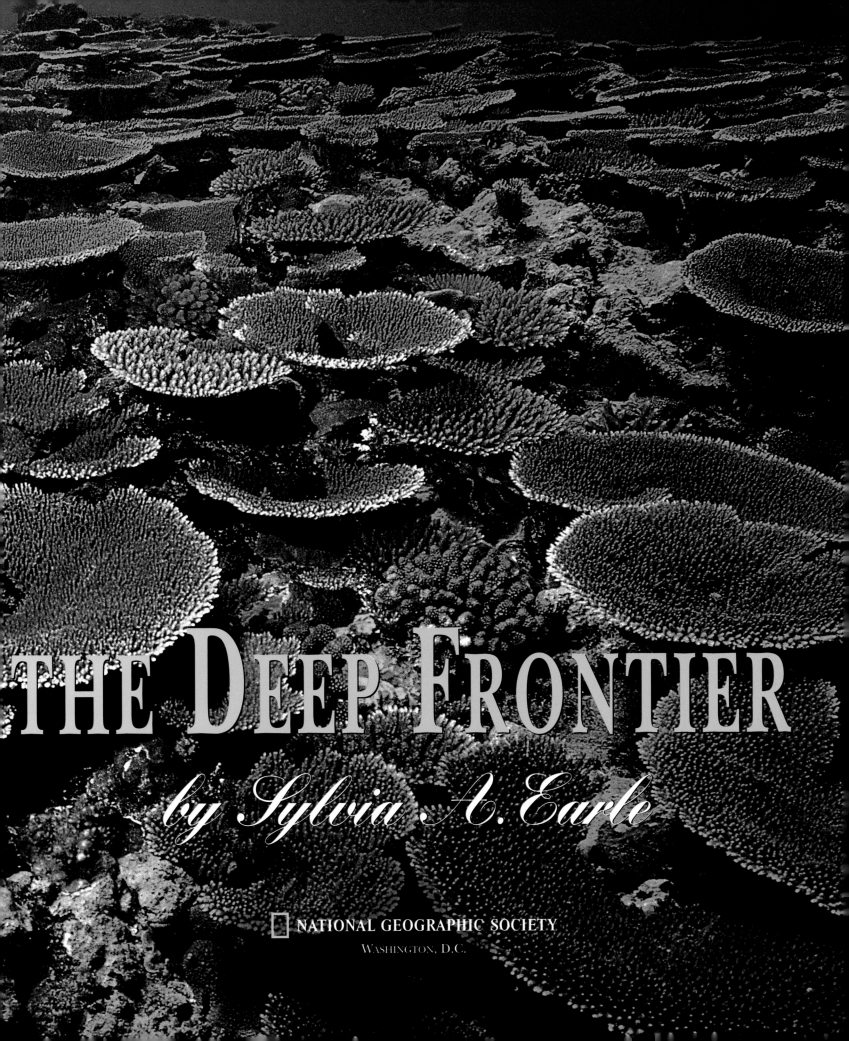

THE DEEP FRONTIER

by Sylvia A. Earle

NATIONAL GEOGRAPHIC SOCIETY

Washington, D.C.

For Taylor, Russell, Kevin, and you, the reader, as you embark on discoveries of your own.

Copyright © 1999 Sylvia A. Earle

All rights reserved. Reproduction of the whole or any part of the contents without written permission from the publisher is prohibited.

Published by the
National Geographic Society
1145 17th Street N.W.
Washington, D.C. 20036

John M. Fahey, Jr.
President and
Chief Executive Officer

Gilbert M. Grosvenor
Chairman of the Board

Nina D. Hoffman
Senior Vice President

William R. Gray
Vice President and Director
of the Book Division

Staff for this book:

Barbara Lalicki
Project Director

Marianne Koszorus
Art Director

David M. Seager
Designer

Suzanne Patrick Fonda
Editor

Jennifer Emmett
Assistant Editor

Carl Mehler
Director of Maps

Elisabeth MacRae-Bobynskyj
Indexer

Vincent P. Ryan
Manufacturing Manager

Lewis Bassford
Production Manager

Library of Congress Cataloging-in-Publication Data

Earle, Sylvia A., 1935–
      Dive! : my adventures in the deep frontier / by Sylvia A. Earle.
               p. cm.
      Includes index.
      Summary: The author relates some of her adventures studying and exploring
the world's oceans, including tracking whales, living in an underwater laboratory, and
helping to design a deep water submarine.
      ISBN 0-7922-7144-0
      1. Undersea Exploration—Juvenile Literature. 2. Deep Diving—Juvenile
Literature.
[1. Underwater exploration. 2. Deep diving. 3. Earle, Sylvia A., 1935– .] I. Title.
GC65.E184 1999
627'7—dc21
                             98–11480

Cover: Sylvia Earle's daughter waves for her mother's camera on a reef in Tonga.

Back cover: Sylvia Earle poses in the submersible, *Deep Worker,* the mini-sub she uses to explore U.S. marine sanctuaries as part of the 1998 Sustainable Seas Expeditions.

Title Page: This coral reef in the Cook Islands harbors an abundance and diversity of life comparable to that of a tropical rain forest.

CONTENTS

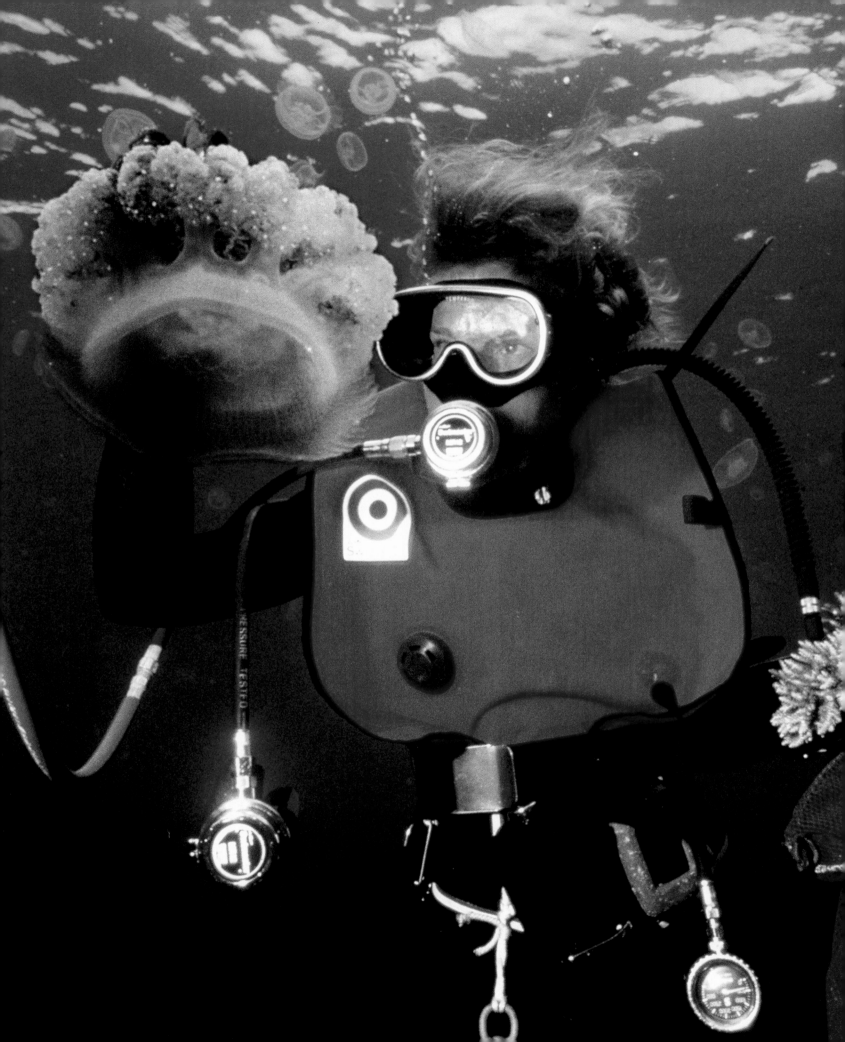

*I*f you want to be the first to go where no one has ever been before, you can. If you want to discover new kinds of animals, new plants, and whole new systems of life, they are there, deep in the sea. You can be the first to explore any of thousands of undersea mountains and cross unknown plains; be the first to figure out how barely known creatures live, how they spend their days and nights, how their lives influence us—and how we who live on the land affect them.

You can also dream up ways to explore the sea—with submersibles, underwater laboratories, robots, new sensors, cameras, and other instruments. If you want to, you can even build your own. I know such things are possible because I have had the fun of doing them and have glimpsed how much more there is to discover.

Sylvia A Earle

Jellies, such as this lacy beauty, collapse into great gobs of goo on the beach. The best way to get to know them and other sea creatures is to go where they live—underwater.

1 GETTING STARTED

My own curiosity about what lives in the sea was sparked during summer vacations with my family along the New Jersey shore. The mysterious creatures I saw at the ocean's edge—glossy brown horseshoe crabs bulldozing their way into wet sand, sandpipers skittering in the surf, and hundreds of tiny translucent sand fleas hopping among hanks of dark seaweed—fascinated me. I read everything I could find about the ocean and wondered what it would be like to swim with dolphins or to meet giant whales eye to eye—underwater. Later, when I was twelve, my family moved to Florida. The clear, warm water of the Gulf of Mexico lapped along the edge of our backyard.

Dolphins sometimes came close to shore, dozens of them. I longed to swim with their grace and speed. I loved their natural ability to see clearly underwater as well as above. I watched the way they breathe—through a single large nostril on the tops of their heads. They did not have to lift their faces out of water to take in air, and I soon found that there was a way for me to do that, too.

Horseshoe crabs—curious "living fossils"—lured me into the sea as a little girl. My friend Elisabeth Polk-Bauman (left) succumbed to their magic appeal at Jamaica Bay, New York.

A cleverly curved tube—a snorkel—made it possible for me to keep my face down but draw in air from above the water's surface. I found that I could inhale deeply through a snorkel and hold my breath for about a minute while swimming underwater before racing back to the surface for more air. To protect my eyes from the burning sting of salt water, I learned to use a diving mask, an oval piece of glass rimmed with soft rubber and held in place by a strap around my head.

Here, my daughter Gale is learning to swim with a mask and snorkel, just as I did as a child.

Creatures such as these beautiful grunts (right), serenely swimming along a coral reef in the Bahamas, made me wish for gills!

Sunlight
Zone

Twilight
Zone

Midnight
Zone

Trench
Zone

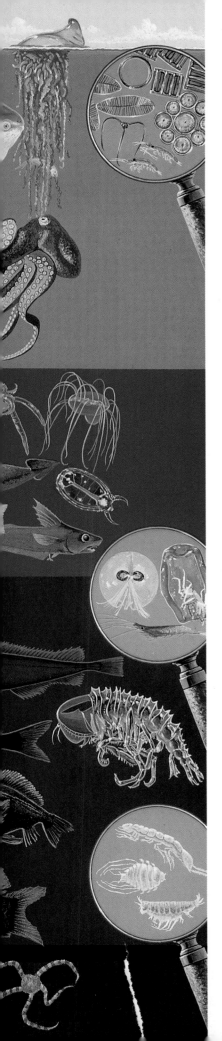

Whales can hold their breath much longer than humans can—sometimes for as much as an hour at a time. I did not hesitate when I first had a chance to use scuba—self-contained underwater breathing apparatus, developed in the 1940s by Jacques Cousteau and Emile Gagnan. Using air tanks with a regulator and a mouthpiece that deliver compressed air on demand, it was possible for me to stay underwater as long as whales do!

With my first breath I swallowed a little salt water, but I could get air even though my head and body were completely submerged. I adjusted my bite on the mouthpiece, took a second breath, then another, and soon forgot about breathing, because it was so easy, and concentrated on looking at a small yellowish brown fish—a grunt—that clearly was looking at me.

I'm not sure what my reaction would be if a great, bubbling creature a hundred times my size suddenly landed in my "backyard," but the small grunt I greeted during my first scuba dive merely regarded me with

I was surprised when a squid I was observing (above) began observing me.

This painting shows the amazing diversity of life in the sea. Very little light reaches beyond 1,000 feet; most of the ocean is deep, dark, and cold. Magnifying glasses reveal some of the smallest creatures. (No life-forms or zones are drawn to scale.)

13

something like mild curiosity. He hunkered down a little among the branches of a tube sponge, and I moved on, delighted with my ability to remain underwater—and to feel weightless.

On land I had, as a child, mastered the fine art of standing on my head, but here I could stand on one finger. I could do loop-de-loops, back rolls, or simply hover, mid-water, like a jellyfish. Time passed much too swiftly, and when my hour was up, I had to climb back in the boat and become an upright primate again. But in my mind I had been transformed irreversibly into a sea creature who henceforth would spend part of the time above water.

I still hoped to meet whales underwater, and after going to school and training to be a scientist, I got my chance.

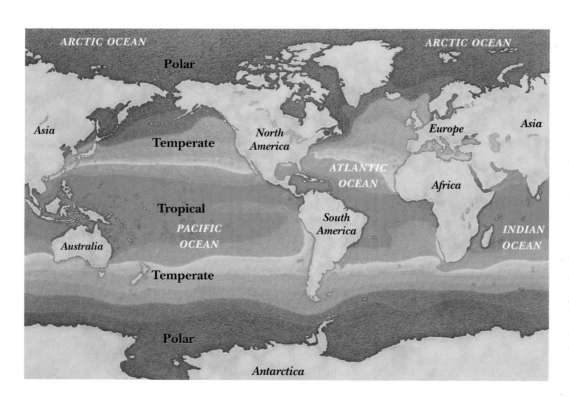

This map shows zones of ocean surface temperatures. Temperature plays a major role in determining where plants and animals live in the ocean.

Sometimes I dream of flying—of gliding wherever I wish, like a bird, like a fish. In the sea the dream comes true.

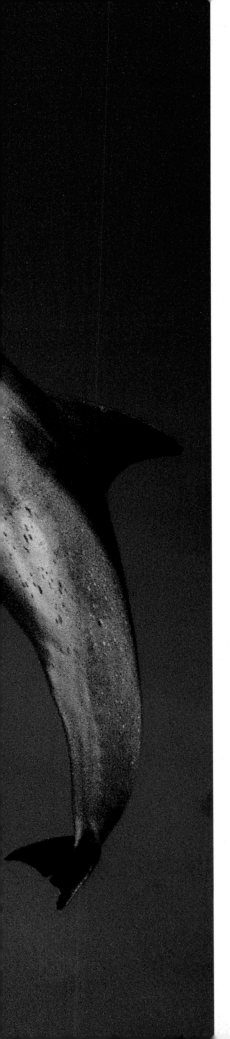

2 EYE TO EYE

I was floating in clear, warm water along the coast of Maui, one of the Hawaiian Islands. Far below was the largest creature I had ever seen—a female humpback whale. She looked as big as a bus and was heading straight toward me. It was too late to worry about whether or not I was in her way or if whales have brakes.

A moment later her grapefruit-size eyes met mine. She tilted right, then left, as her 15-foot flippers and powerful tail propelled her past me far faster than humans can swim or run. I glanced at my own slip-on flippers, a wonderful aid for human feet underwater but no match for a whale's built-in propulsion system. As she swam away, I could see how huge she really was—40 feet long and probably weighing 40 tons! We named her Daisy because of the flowerlike pattern on her tail.

I had come to Hawaii with a small team of scientists and photographers to observe whales underwater. From the start I found myself being observed by them. Daisy and four companions circled around me gracefully as I tried to identify them. Photographer Al Giddings was

Looking into the eyes of a wild dolphin—who is looking into mine—inspires me to learn everything I can about them and do everything I can to take care of them.

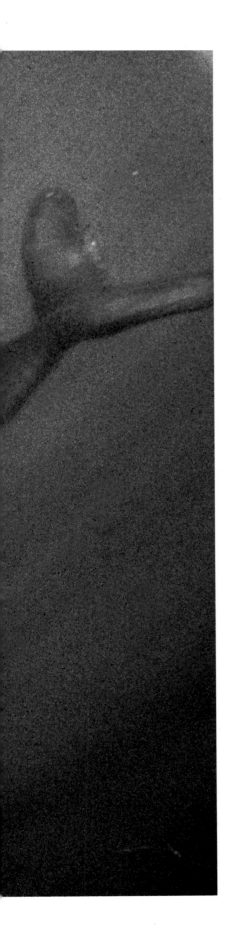

working nearby, and I watched as a whale artfully lifted her flipper to avoid colliding with him. These huge creatures have an easy command of their big bodies and seem to have no desire to harm humans in their midst.

At this time (in the 1970s) most of what was known about whales had been discovered by studying their dead bodies. Tags embedded in the backs of whales were recovered when the whales were killed, and from these, information was gained about how far they travel and how long they live.

Zoologists Roger Payne and Katy Payne, who were studying the sounds and songs of humpback whales, were among the scientists who inspired me to try to get to know whales on their own terms. The examples of Jane Goodall, Dian Fossey, and George Schaller, who were studying animals on their home ground, also inspired me to see whales in their natural habitat.

"Home" for whales is a place several thousand miles long, with the dining room at one end in cool, northern waters and the nursery at the other in the tropics.

In Hawaii Al and I were in the nursery, trying to see if we could record the short grunts and squeals associated with certain whale behaviors. The Paynes had given us suggestions about how to do this.

It might seem easy, but when swimming underwater, it is almost impossible to determine the direction sounds are coming from. Often, many whales are vocalizing at once, and the sounds may travel many miles.

In the weeks that followed we heard whales singing day and night, and once while underwater, whalesong was so loud that the air spaces in my body vibrated— a feeling something like being next to a very loud drum

Whales, such as this 40-foot-long humpback, are masters of diving. We have much to learn by observing them in their own realm.

At the surface, bubble nets blown by feeding humpback whales appear as sizzling circles surrounding large masses of krill. These two whales in Glacier Bay, Alaska, have just gulped down thousands of the tiny creatures.

or in the midst of an orchestra. The whale was close but not close enough for me to see. Al was the first to find and film one—a lone male, repeating deep rumbling rolls and high birdlike trills.

That summer Al Giddings and I went to the whales' dining room—the plankton-rich waters of Glacier Bay, Alaska. The bay water was a murky green, filled with billions of small plants, or plankton, that shrimplike krill dine on. I did not find Daisy, but I did see dozens of humpback whales who'd traveled from tropical seas to feast on the krill. Scientist Charles "Chuck" Jurasz had

observed whales blowing huge circles of bubbles then exploding upward through the center of the ring, mouths wide open—an apparent strategy for "netting" krill and getting a good meal! Al and I wanted to document this bubblenet feeding phenomenon, so we went out with Chuck on his boat, *Ginjur*.

To get a closer view Al and I left *Ginjur* and loaded our gear into a small rubber boat. Perched in the bow of our tiny craft, Al was able to film the whales blowing bubbles and gulping krill at such close range that we often got sprayed with krill-perfumed whale breath.

From afar, scientist Chuck Jurasz and I watch as a tail of a familiar humpback whale disappears under the surface of Glacier Bay.

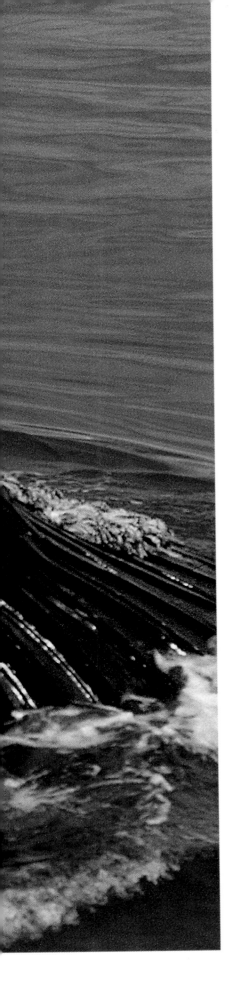

Once, a solitary whale blew circle after circle of bubbles, each time lunging precisely through the center, his huge mouth spilling out hundreds of gallons of water while straining out the tasty morsels of krill. Then, the whale dived down near our small boat, and we watched spellbound as a circle of bubbles formed right around us! There wasn't time to move. We just held on, caught in the bubble net....

Perhaps the sound of bubbles breaking on the bottom of our boat stopped the whale. All we know for sure is that, as we held our breath expecting to be eaten, the whale surfaced a few feet away—mouth closed. He exhaled a mighty *whoosh* of air and dived back into the water.

A century ago people from many nations were killing large numbers of whales because the fatty blubber that keeps whales warm was a good source of oil for lamps. Some people also ate whale meat and used their bones for tools. Nothing in the millions of years of whale history prepared them to cope with humans as predators, especially when we began using swift boats and harpoon

Hungry humpbacks (left) strain inch-long crustaceans called krill (above) from Alaskan waters.

guns equipped with explosives. Within a few decades so many whales had been killed that the number of some kinds declined to very low levels.

People all over the world now recognize the importance of whales for something more than a meal, and most nations have stopped killing them. Some engineers regard whales as priceless sources of information about the optimum shapes and designs for submarines and other equipment that must move underwater. Scientists are learning how whales communicate and navigate over thousands of miles without maps, and how they manage to withstand great pressure while holding

their breath during especially deep dives.

Many people simply delight in getting to know whales as I have—eye to eye, one on one—and wish to protect them as magnificent treasures, easy to kill but impossible to replace once gone.

The black-and-white pattern on every humpback whale's tail is as distinctive as a fingerprint, so a collection of whale-tail photographs makes it possible to figure out which whales are where.

3 GOING DEEPER

With scuba I explored the Gulf of Mexico—underwater—starting with the beautiful sea-grass meadows that border much of the western Florida shoreline. Among vast aquatic fields of grasslike plants that have flowers (turtle grass, manatee grass, reef grass, and others) were algae, nonflowering plants that I thought were irresistible. There were nearly 100 kinds of green algae, 75 or so species of brown algae (so called for their distinctive yellow-brown pigments), and more than 300 kinds of pale pink to deep ruby-colored plants known generally as red algae.

I love to explore coral reefs (left) and study the plants that grow among the colorful animals that live there. This encrusting red alga (above) is one of many plants that extract calcium carbonate—limestone— from seawater. Such plants are important reef builders.

In Indian Ocean coral reefs I found creatures that looked a lot like those in the Gulf of Mexico, but the individual species were different. For instance, both places had parrotfish, puffers, surgeonfish, barracudas, and sharks, but their colors and spots and shapes were different in the same way that lions and tigers and panthers are all obviously cats, but each has its own special features that set it apart from others of the same family. This was true of the plants, too.

Seahorse

Spotted pufferfish

Lionfish

Arrow crab

These are among the thousands of sea creatures who have allowed me to spend time with them.

Here (right), I share a book about fish with yellowtail snappers, parrotfish, and others.

These creole wrasses cruising a Caribbean reef are part of the intricate web of life in the sea. Fish are distinctly different from each other, just as are cats, dogs, horses, and birds.

Scientists who want to study forests, deserts, or mountains and the plants and animals that live there can drive to their favorite places and spend hours walking around, waiting for just the right actions to occur. With scuba, time is limited not only by the amount of air in the tank but also by the gases in air—oxygen and nitrogen—that can cause problems when breathed under pressure.

It is important to ascend slowly after diving with compressed air. Coming up too fast, especially when you have been diving deep or for a long time, causes a reaction something like what happens when you take the top off a bottle of soda. Rapid release of pressure causes a fizz of bubbles. That's all right for soda, but bubbles in your bloodstream can cause the bends, a reaction that is painful and sometimes fatal unless you take time to slowly allow the nitrogen in your system to dissipate. The process is called decompression.

The amount of time you can spend without decompression decreases the deeper you go. It is possible to spend about an hour 50 feet down without taking time to decompress. At 100 feet it is possible to stay less than half an hour; at 150 feet you have about 10 minutes. Even though the time is short, it is longer than what is possible just holding your breath. I thoroughly enjoyed hundreds of hours getting acquainted with creatures who live not far from shore but who are unknown to most people.

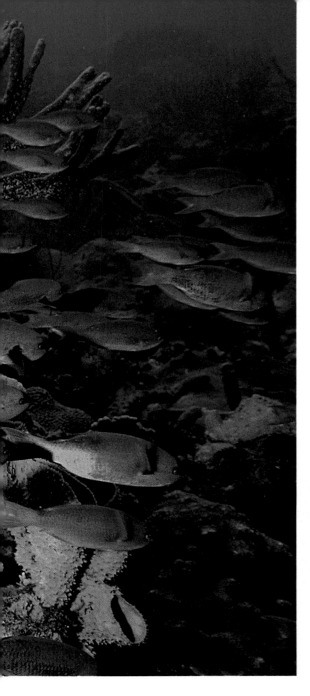

Using nets to catch samples, scientists can learn a lot about what creatures live in the sea but little about how they live, what they do, or how many are there.

Sometimes we used nets and small boxlike devices to gather samples, especially in water deeper than we could dive in using scuba. The nets were towed along the seafloor or mid-water, sometimes for more than an hour before they were brought back to the surface using powerful winches. As the catch spilled out on the deck—usually a confusing mix of starfish, seaweed, mollusks, crabs, fish, sponges, bits of coral, chunks of rock, and much more—I wondered what aliens exploring Earth might think of us and our cities if they used only nets to capture random bits and pieces of buildings, shrubs, cats, dogs, people, cars, and sidewalks squished together and dragged around for a while before being emptied in a heap.

What could they discover about how we live or what we do? How could they know that we have voices and names and music and laughter? And what, I wondered, can we know about the creatures in the sea if we never go there ourselves? The difference between the crushed and mangled samples that came up in nets and what I knew was below from having been there myself made me determined to concentrate on the direct approach—to go underwater. I wondered, what would Jane Goodall know of chimpanzees if she had studied them only by flying over forests in a helicopter, snagging them in a net?

Some scientists were skeptical about the use of scuba for scientific exploration. A few even suggested that diving was too much fun to be taken seriously by scientists. But for me, science is fun! I already knew how important diving can be as a way to observe life in the sea directly. I use scuba in the same way I use microscopes and other equipment—as a tool that makes it possible to explore.

The biggest problems with scuba diving were that I could not go as deep or stay as long as I wanted to. I dreamed of being able to live under the sea.

Using scuba I can spend hours with some of my favorite fish. This one, a Nassau grouper on a reef in the Bahamas, reminds me of a friendly puppy.

4 STAYING LONGER

y dream of staying underwater for days at a time came true in a spectacular way.

I was selected to become an aquanaut to head the first team of women who would live in an underwater laboratory called Tektite for two weeks. In addition to scuba we'd use special equipment called rebreathers to explore and study the reefs. Like the life-support system of astronauts, the rebreathers aquanauts use recycle air over and over, removing carbon dioxide chemically and automatically adding oxygen from a special tank as needed.

Like an underwater space station, the Tektite laboratory (left) was my home on a reef for two weeks with the fish and my team- mates Peggy Lucas, Ann Hurley, Renata True, and Alina Szmant (above, left to right). I'm on the far right.

Located just offshore in Great Lameshur Bay, St. John Island in the U.S. Virgin Islands, the Tektite laboratory seemed to defy the laws of nature.

Imagine sitting warm and dry at a table 50 feet underwater, munching on a sandwich, and talking with your friends while fish peer in the window! Imagine washing the dishes, then taking off your T-shirt and shorts, putting on a bathing suit, flippers, mask, and air tank, then stepping through a round hole in the floor and swimming off into the sea. That's what my four companions and I did several times a day for two weeks in 1970.

Peggy Lucas, an engineer from the University of Delaware who looked after the functioning of the laboratory, was my main diving buddy. We often got up before dawn to be on the reef when the sun came up. We took note of which fish were the early risers and which ones liked to sleep in. Some, like parrotfish, surgeonfish, and wrasses, are active all day and tuck into crevices and crannies at night. Usually the same fish returns to its special place night after night. Other fish rest during the day— sometimes in the very same crevices vacated by night-sleepers.

Dawn and dusk are great times to watch the changeover between creatures active at different times and to see which fish are solitary, which ones join up with others, and whether or not the same fish get together repeatedly as their day—or night—begins. I wanted to find out which plants parrotfish and other grazers eat and to inventory all of the species of fish and plants I could find around the reef and learn whatever I could about their behavior.

I discovered that fish, like people, have food preferences. Some damselfish even establish and maintain gardens of the plants they like to eat! Damselfish weed out plants they don't like and use the weeded patches as nurseries for clusters of eggs. When the young hatch, food and shelter are right

This round opening in the floor was the entrance to our undersea home. Air pressure kept the ocean from flooding in.

there, with fiercely protective parents close by.

Parrotfish have teeth that are fused into sharp, beaklike plates just right for scraping and biting seaweed from the surface of dead coral and rocks. As they munch, their noisy *snap-crunch-crunch-crrrrunch* sounds like my brothers eating carrots and celery. But not all parrotfish like to eat the same things. Some, I discovered, have a decided preference for the tender tips of *Halimeda* plants; others spurn *Halimeda* but nibble on fuzzy clusters of green, red, and blue-green algae.

None of the more than 30 kinds of fish in this area that include plants in their diet seemed to like any of the bright green fronds of plants called *Caulerpa*. I wondered why, because *Caulerpa* looks rather appealing, and in

Parrotfish, such as this beauty, use their beaklike mouths to bite and scrape seaweed from coral. Curiously, they usually avoid Caulerpa, *the green mushroomlike plants on the right.*

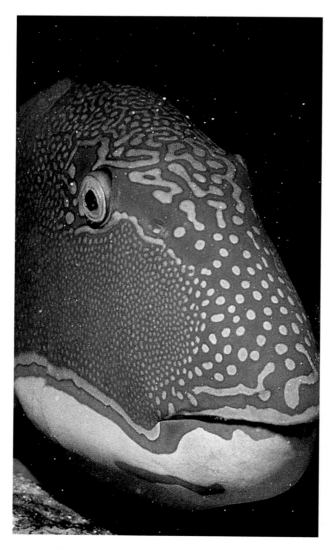

some parts of the world people serve it in salad. I sampled some myself and decided that the fish were right. Salty and slightly bitter, species of *Caulerpa* have a successful and untasty strategy for survival.

Living underwater has many advantages, but most important is the gift of time. We could and often did make long excursions to depths more than 100 feet. We spent as much as 12 hours a day in the water, taking time out now and then to eat and sleep or examine special things using microscopes that were inside the laboratory. Of course, at the end of our mission underwater we had to decompress. It took 19 hours in a special chamber to safely and slowly return to surface pressure, but it was worth it to have

Halimeda *(left), a kind of plant that is common on coral reefs, is often trimmed by grazing fish. My friend Kimeo Aisek (above) discovered what fish seem to know: Some plants taste awful.*

A fish-eye view shows a diver entering Aquarius, an underwater laboratory in the Florida Keys National Marine Sanctuary.

extended time completely submerged for two weeks.

In 1996 I joined a group of five other scientists in a modern underwater laboratory called Aquarius. Located on a coral reef in the midst of the Florida Keys National Marine Sanctuary, five miles offshore near Key Largo, Aquarius has been a place where geologists, chemists, biologists, and others have come to study the reefs.

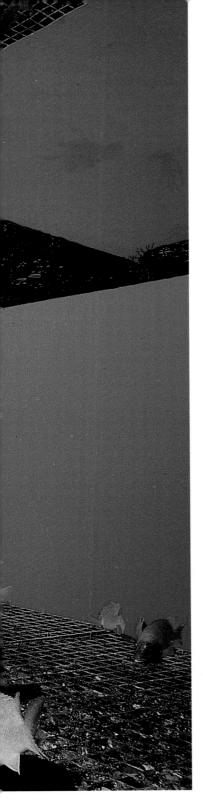

In recent years many of the reefs have become diseased, and some are dying. I wanted to help find out why and see if there are ways to stop the decline and restore damaged systems. There seems to be a correlation between troubled reefs and increased pollution from cities and farms in central and south Florida and the Keys, coupled with greatly increased shoreline activity—marinas, houses, roads, and more. Much more needs to be learned about what keeps corals healthy and what causes them to die, but the idea of exploring and protecting the reefs in the Florida Keys seems very wise. Like whales, coral reefs are easy to kill but impossible to replace once they are gone.

One underwater laboratory—Hydrolab—has been my home-on-a-reef at a site a mile offshore from Freeport, on Grand Bahama Island. Hydrolab is a one-room, four-

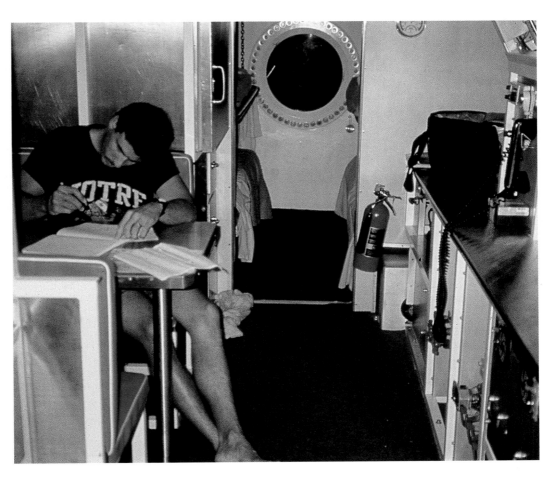

Inside Aquarius an aquanaut sits warm, dry, and comfortable 60 feet under the sea!

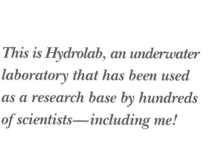

This is Hydrolab, an underwater laboratory that has been used as a research base by hundreds of scientists—including me!

bunk system. Housekeeping and meal preparation are very simple—rather like camping, with freeze-dried food, crunchy cereal, and lots of peanut butter to eat.

I wanted to find out how deep in the sea plants can grow. Not surprisingly, plankton is concentrated in the well-illuminated uppermost part of the water. Photosynthesis—the process whereby green plants transform carbon dioxide and water into simple sugar and oxygen—is utterly dependent on light. But how much light is needed? After all, most of the yellow and red light from the sun is absorbed in the upper few feet of seawater. Light waves at the far blue end of the spectrum penetrate farther. I wanted to know if the books that claim plants can live no deeper than 300 feet were right. There were reports of plants growing much deeper, but no one knew how deep.

During one stay in Hydrolab I had a chance to try to find out by using an unusual submarine, the *Johnson Sea Link*. I swam over and climbed into it. We closed the hatch and the sub's pilot, Tim Askew, drove to the edge of a steep underwater cliff. He stopped at 250 feet—the maximum depth I was allowed to go while breathing compressed air. Gliding out of the sub, I was free to explore for almost an hour.

On a ledge along the cliff I spotted a miniature green forest of plants unlike any I had ever seen before, either in books or in the sea. Since I was the first to find this kind of plant, I had the fun of naming it and chose *Johnson-sea-linkia profunda* in honor of the submarine. A few days later, other forests of the newly discovered plant

*This **Johnson Sea Link** submarine is used like an underwater taxi to transport scientists to deep water. The pilot and an observer sit up front in the clear sphere. Divers can swim out of a special compartment in the back of the sub.*

were observed from the *Johnson Sea Link* in 500 to 600 feet of water—about twice as deep as some people thought possible. Sometime later in the Bahamas, scientists Diane Littler and Mark Littler traveled in the *Johnson Sea Link* and found red algae growing at 878 feet. The maximum depth for plants living and photosynthesizing in the sea is still not known, but the Littlers and I will keep looking.

ONWARD & DOWNWARD

*L*ike a hawk gliding, I swam in clear blue water far offshore in the Bahama Islands. A large Nassau grouper circled around me, his great brown eyes meeting mine. Then, with a gentle flip of his tail, he swam down into an underwater canyon. I longed to follow but looked at my watch and depth gauge. I was 120 feet down and had been underwater for 15 minutes. If I stayed longer, I would have to decompress—stopping along the way back to allow compressed nitrogen that had accumulated in my blood-stream to gradually dissipate. My air supply was too limited for me to take the time needed to do that, so with a sigh, I turned back toward the surface. I dreamed of finding a way to go really deep into the sea.

Soon after, I heard about a special diving suit called Jim. It looks like the suits astronauts wear in space. Commercial divers use it for underwater salvage operations and to maintain oil rigs. I thought it could also be used for scientists to explore and conduct research.

Jim was named for the first person willing to try it— Jim Jarrett. In a special training tank in southern California I learned how to climb in and out of the thousand-pound suit, how to put on the helmet, and how to move.

In this diving suit, called Jim, I descended 1,250 feet from sunlight into darkness. On the bottom, I stepped off the platform attached to the little submarine Star II.

At sea level the weight of the atmosphere above puts 14.7 pounds of pressure on every square inch of whatever is below—including us. That pressure, "one atmosphere," is doubled 33 feet underwater and increases by 14.7 pounds per square inch, or another atmosphere of pressure for every additional 33 feet of descent. Inside Jim the pressure is always the same as it is at the surface: one atmosphere.

After weeks of preparation the time came to test the concept of using Jim for research.

Strapped to the front of a little submarine, *Star II*, I descended inside Jim through the brightly illuminated surface to intensely blue depths that finally merged with black. At 1,250 feet the sub and I landed with a gentle bump. A strap that held me in place was released.

I stepped into a forest of whisker-like bamboo coral. Lights from the little submarine beamed on a pink sea fan, and I watched as bright red crabs swam to it and hung on like shirts drying in a deep-sea wind. A great

*To enter Jim (above), I climbed in from the top. Then, strapped to a platform attached to the **Star II** sub, I descended to the ocean floor. To return to the surface (right), the **Star II** sub ascended, towing me with it.*

pale crab as large as a cat crept into the light, then paused to look at a strange joint-legged creature unlike anything it had ever encountered before—me.

In some ways I might as well have been on the moon, but there are no lacy pink corals, bright red crabs, or crabs that look like cats on the moon.

There may be living creatures elsewhere in the universe, perhaps even on Mars where water once abounded. Maybe there is life on Europa, one of Jupiter's moons where an ocean has been discovered. But we know of nowhere else, not even in the richest rain forests of our planet, where there is greater diversity of animals, plants, and microbial life than in Earth's vast saltwater realm.

More than 30 major divisions of animals are known, and all have some representation in the sea: from sponges and jellies to many kinds of beautiful worms and mollusks; from starfish and their relatives to moss animals, lamp shells, and creatures with backbones— fish, turtles, whales, and even diving seabirds. Only about half of these categories of life occur on land, but on a single dive I often encounter more than two dozen.

Although I was excited by explorations that could be made with Jim, I wondered, why stop at 1,250 feet? The ocean, after all, has an average depth of two and a half miles, more than 13,000 feet. Why not have one-atmosphere diving systems like Jim that can go all the way to the deepest part of the ocean: to the bottom of the Mariana Trench, east of the Philippine Islands— seven miles down?

It is amazing that only two people in all of the history of humankind have been there. Their diving system was the bathyscaphe *Trieste*. Their historic dive took place in 1960—nine years before the first humans landed on the moon. Since then dozens of people have left Earth's atmosphere as astronauts, instruments have landed on

Like an alien spacecraft, this jellyfish pulses through the sea.

Mars, and cameras in deep space have inspected the outer reaches of the solar system. Meanwhile, no one has returned to the deepest sea, and no submersibles exist now that can take us there and back.

I wanted to explore the deepest parts of the ocean, but *Trieste* no longer was being used. To do what I wanted to do would take something new.

I described the problem to an engineer friend, Graham Hawkes, who had helped modernize Jim for work on offshore oil rigs. At first he told me why my "dream sub" wasn't possible.

Like birds in a forest, blue damselfish flit among the tangled branches of a sponge off Bonaire, in the Netherlands Antilles.

"Pressure is the biggest problem," he said. "You could build a submersible out of a metal such as steel or titanium. Both are strong, but not transparent. Also, to go deep the best shape isn't something that fits over arms and legs like Jim does. A sphere is ideal because pressure is equally distributed overall.

"Glass would be wonderful to use because you would be inside a clear bubble; you wouldn't need to have windows. You could use a kind of clear acrylic plastic—the same stuff that is used to make the thick windows in the giant fish tanks in aquariums."

We talked about other problems. Light penetrates underwater only a few hundred feet in many coastal areas, and even in very clear water it is completely dark below about 1,500 feet. I wanted to go much deeper than that and be able to dive at night when many special creatures are most active.

"Even with lights," Graham reminded me, "it's not possible to see very far underwater. You should have an acoustic system—sonar—like dolphins and whales have naturally so you can 'see' with sound."

"That's easy to add," I said. "What else do we have to worry about?"

"To be safe, you should have an extra air supply, and what about arms? Those on Jim won't work below about 1,500 feet. What about having mechanical arms?"

The more we talked, the more real the idea became.

In my dream machine, the submersible **Deep Rover,** *I explored deep reefs in the Bahamas.*

The first step would be to start with a basic design. Building a small, clear, spherical submersible with mechanical arms and a generous supply of air seemed a logical place to begin.

Deep Rover soon became more than a dream.

Graham and I started a submarine company and found an ally in a fellow explorer, Phil Nuytten. Four years and a lot of hard work later, I looked through the clear, curved acrylic dome of the first *Deep Rover.* Our company, Deep Ocean Engineering, built the little sub; Phil's company, Can Dive Services, owned it. Graham, Phil, and I were the first to use it for its deepest dives— to 3,000 feet. There was still a long way to go to get seven miles down, but we were heading in the right direction.

As I descended into a dark sea several miles offshore from San Diego, California, thousands of small creatures flowing over *Deep Rover*'s sphere sparkled with blue-green light. Like falling into a galaxy, I thought. I was alone as a human being but surrounded by living things whose existence was unknown to most of my species.

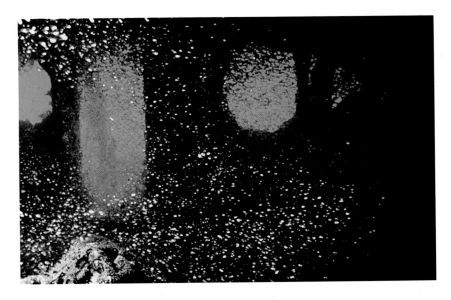

New diving techniques make it possible to explore sunken ships, such as this one (above) glistening with silver fish at the bottom of Truk Lagoon, in Micronesia. Lights from a submersible illuminate a deep reef in the Bahamas (left).

53

I reached overhead to turn a valve that adjusted *Deep Rover*'s buoyancy and for a while simply hovered, neither rising nor falling—much like one of the gelatinous creatures I had come to see. With the lights on I could see tiny jellies, small shrimp, the glint of silver from a curious fish, and the translucent form of a speckled octopus clinging to the outside of the sphere. With the lights off I could see showers of bioluminescence as creatures brushed by—small jewel-like ingredients in a vast, living soup. Again adjusting buoyancy, I continued downward, wondering what might be in the depths below.

As I neared maximum depth, I turned on the sub's lights and could see soft, brown mud marked with the burrows and mounds of numerous creatures who make their homes in the seafloor. I tried to land gently so as not to disturb the local residents, and as I did, something on the bottom seemed to flash in the sub's lights—something silvery with a reddish glint.

Cautiously, I moved closer, hoping I wouldn't startle the strange creature. Many deep-sea fish move slowly, and most would likely be stunned by the unfamiliar glare of lights from the sub. This whatever-it-was did not move, and I carefully reached forward with the manipulator. The silvery red, sparkling object remained motionless, and I held my breath and tilted the lights to a new angle. Suddenly I knew what it was. A soda can!

It was not really a surprise. Whatever gets tossed into the sea doesn't just go away; it settles down in some other place, out of sight but not really gone. Some bits of junk are quietly being transformed into homes for sponges and small fish, like miniature shipwrecks in the sea, but I felt like apologizing on behalf of my species for raining debris on the unsuspecting communities of life in the deep.

Inside a two-person **Deep Rover II,** *I viewed marine life among California's Channel Islands.*

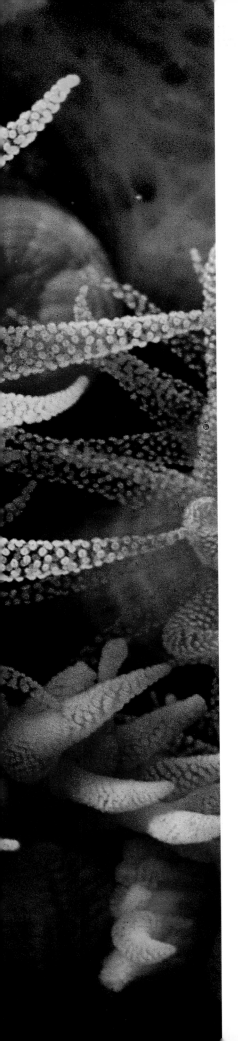

6 OCEAN CARE

*A*fter many dives in many places it seems to me that, in general, using the ocean as a place to dump things we do not want on the land is not the right way to go. Under the sea as well as on beaches everywhere, debris is accumulating that can be deadly. An osprey hopelessly tangled in discarded fishing line once landed in a tree in my mother's yard in Florida—a victim of someone's carelessness. The bird's fierce will to live despite its terrible wounds became, for me, one of the

We can choose to keep the ocean safe for marine creatures, such as this magnificent coral (left), or trash their future—and ours (above).

thousands of reasons why it is vital to understand the consequences of what we thoughtlessly put into the sea.

Lots of things we do can harm the ocean. Taking too much wildlife out of the sea is one way. Putting garbage, toxic chemicals, and other wastes in is another. But underlying all of the problems is the most serious issue—ignorance. We must explore to better understand the nature of the oceans and how they work before we do more damage to those systems that are vital to the survival and well-being of humans and the rest of life on Earth. Without the ocean and all of its wondrous life human life would not be possible.

Everyone can help. Everyone can make wise choices about what to eat or not to eat. Everyone can dispose of trash safely. And everyone can help support ideas that will provide protection for the sea. Graham Hawkes and Phil Nuytten design submersibles that take us beneath the sea; Roger Payne, Katy Payne, and Chuck Jurasz learn about whales and share their insights; my mother rescues injured birds. Some people inspire with poetry; others make laws or teach or, like Diane Littler and Mark Littler, study plants. I have embarked on a new project at the National Geographic Society—the Sustainable Seas Expeditions—to dive in *Deep Worker* submersibles throughout the nation's system of marine sanctuaries.

Five centuries ago explorers charted the surface of the sea and got to know the arrangement of the continents for the first time. Almost two centuries ago explorers Meriwether Lewis and William Clark set out to discover what they could about the unknown territory west of the Mississippi River. As we begin a new century, similar challenges await a few feet from any shore.

The greatest era of exploration of this ocean planet has just begun!

There is so much of the ocean still to explore—from coral reefs in the tropics to deep canyons and the more than 40,000 miles of mountain ranges that spring from the seafloor.

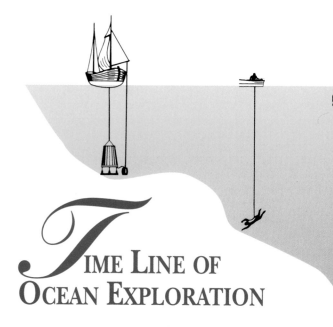

TIME LINE OF OCEAN EXPLORATION

Fourth century B.C.
Greek sponge divers breathe air trapped in kettles lowered underwater.

First century B.C.
 Diving women of the northwestern Pacific hold their breath to gather food from the seafloor. Diving women of Japan, called Ama, continue the tradition today.

1690
In England Edmond Halley invents a diving bell which divers later use to descend to more than 50 feet.

1776
First attack by a military submarine.

1800
U.S. inventor Robert Fulton tests his submarine, *Nautilus*, in France.

1839
 The British Royal Navy founds the first diving school at the wreck site of a sunken warship.

1844
Henri Milne-Edwards of France and a naturalist friend conduct the first underwater studies of marine life off Sicily.

1872
H.M.S. *Challenger* begins a three-and-a-half-year worldwide voyage to study the oceans.

1892
Louis Boutan takes the first underwater still photographs off France.

1906
John Haldane of Scotland conducts experiments to establish decompression tables for compressed-air diving to 200 feet.

1926
William H. Longley and NATIONAL GEOGRAPHIC's Charles Martin take the first artificially lighted underwater color photographs off Florida's Dry Tortugas Islands.

1930
Using a bathysphere, naturalist Dr. William Beebe and designer Otis Barton dive to 1,428 feet off Bermuda.

1943
Frenchmen Jacques Cousteau and Emile Gagnan perfect the fully automatic compressed-air Aqua-Lung and use it to dive to 210 feet in the Mediterranean.

1960
In the bathyscaphe *Trieste*, Jacques Piccard and Lt. Don Walsh, USN, descend to 35,800 feet in the Mariana Trench, the deepest known place in the sea.

1962
In a diving project called Man-in-Sea, Belgian Robert Sténuit descends in a decompression chamber to 200 feet off the French Riviera and stays 24 hours.

1964
Four U.S. Navy divers stay 11 days at 193 feet off Bermuda in Sealab I.

1967
Edwin A. Link builds *Deep Diver*, the first modern submersible with an operational lock-out chamber.

1968
Hydrolab is launched in Florida and begins more than two decades of research by teams of four scientists who spend seven to ten days living and working underwater.

1969
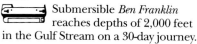 Submersible *Ben Franklin* reaches depths of 2,000 feet in the Gulf Stream on a 30-day journey.

1970
Eleven teams of five people, including one all-women team, each spend from 14 to 20 days at 50 feet off the U.S. Virgin Islands in the underwater laboratory Tektite.

1976
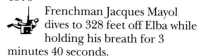 Frenchman Jacques Mayol dives to 328 feet off Elba while holding his breath for 3 minutes 40 seconds.

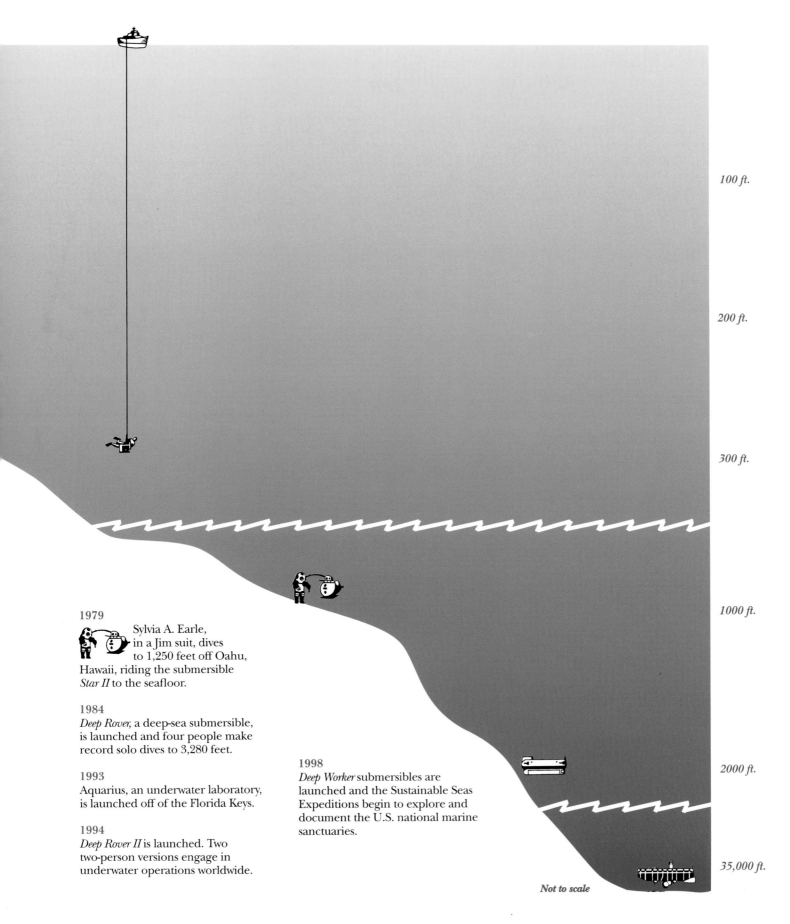

100 ft.

200 ft.

300 ft.

1000 ft.

1979
Sylvia A. Earle, in a Jim suit, dives to 1,250 feet off Oahu, Hawaii, riding the submersible *Star II* to the seafloor.

1984
Deep Rover, a deep-sea submersible, is launched and four people make record solo dives to 3,280 feet.

1993
Aquarius, an underwater laboratory, is launched off of the Florida Keys.

1994
Deep Rover II is launched. Two two-person versions engage in underwater operations worldwide.

1998
Deep Worker submersibles are launched and the Sustainable Seas Expeditions begin to explore and document the U.S. national marine sanctuaries.

2000 ft.

35,000 ft.

Not to scale

GLOSSARY

algae
plant or plantlike organisms usually found in water and commonly distinguished by color: green, red, yellow-green, brown, and blue-green

ama
a Japanese diver, especially for pearls

aquanaut
a scuba diver who lives and operates both inside and outside an underwater shelter for an extended period

bathyscaphe
a special submersible built for deep-sea exploration with a spherical watertight cabin

bathysphere
a round steel diving device

bends
a sometimes fatal condition marked by pain, paralysis, and breathing distress due to the release of nitrogen bubbles in the bloodstream caused by too sudden a change in pressure, as when a diver ascends rapidly from the compressed atmosphere of the deep sea

bioluminescence
the emission of light from living organisms

blubber
the fat of whales and other large marine mammals

bubblenet feeding
a feeding technique of whales in which a whale blows bubbles from underwater to trap krill, then gulps them in as it swims to the surface.

calcium carbonate
a mineral that is the main ingredient of limestone

compressed air
air under pressure greater than that of the atmosphere, as in a scuba tank

decompression
a release from pressure

dolphin
a kind of small, toothed whale

Gulf Stream
a warm ocean current that sweeps north from the Caribbean Sea along the U.S. coast and moves east across the North Atlantic Ocean

krill
a type of shrimplike crustacean that is the main food of certain whales

lock-out chamber
A pressurized chamber that enables divers to transfer from a sub into the sea and back again

Mariana Trench
deepest known depression in the ocean floor

mouthpiece
the part of scuba gear that is inserted into the mouth to supply air to a diver underwater

photosynthesis
the process by which green plants use energy from sunlight to combine water and carbon dioxide to make food and oxygen

plankton
the tiny animals and plants that drift about in huge groups in the surface waters of the ocean.

rebreathers
devices that recycle air for aquanauts by removing carbon dioxide chemically and adding oxygen from a tank as needed

regulator
a device that controls the amount of compressed air a diver breathes in while swimming underwater

salps
a kind of deep-sea animal, usually transparent with a barrel shape

saturation
the point when tissues have fully absorbed gases at a given pressure

scuba
(self-contained underwater breathing apparatus) gear that draws on a portable compressed-air supply at a regulated pressure to allow a diver to breathe while underwater

snorkel
a tube that extends above water and makes it possible for a person to breathe while swimming facedown in the water

submersible
a small underwater craft used especially for deep-sea research

temperate
term for waters with generally moderate year-round temperatures that lie between the Tropic of Cancer and the Arctic Circle or between the Tropic of Capricorn and the Antarctic Circle

titanium
a lightweight metal valued for its strength and resistance to rust, especially from seawater

translucent
clear, transparent; lets light shine through

tropics
a region with generally warm year-round temperatures that extends from the Equator north to the Tropic of Cancer and south to the Tropic of Capricorn

ACKNOWLEDGMENTS

For me as a child, the National Geographic Society's magazine was a window on wild places that I longed to see for myself. The stories there made me dream that I, too, might someday climb into a submarine or "fly" underwater with a scuba tank on my back. So, first I want to thank the National Geographic Society for its long tradition of exploration and for its support of my adventures, including this book, with a special bow to Barbara Lalicki, Jennifer Emmett, Suzanne Fonda, and Tom Powell who worked closely with me to assemble the words and images here.

I am grateful to my parents for inspiring in me and many others the sense of wonder, curiosity, respect, and care for wild places and wild creatures that I have tried to convey in this book. Also, I want to thank my children—Elizabeth, Richie, and Gale—for sharing with me their views of the world and for continuing the ethic of their grandparents.

Some of us are lucky enough to have a special friend or teacher who helps shape the way forward. For me, Harold J. Humm was and still is that person. It was he who first strapped a scuba tank on my back; I was 17 years old. Special thanks are due also to Al Giddings, who not only provided many photographs for this book but also shared with me some of the most extraordinary moments described.

Finally, I want to thank Gardiner Greene Hubbard for his thoughts in the NATIONAL GEOGRAPHIC, Volume 1, Number 1, 1888. They're still right on the mark...

"When we embark on the great ocean of discovery, the horizon of the unknown advances with us wherever we go. The more we know, the greater we find is our ignorance."

Resources
National Geographic Society
c/o Sustainable Seas Expeditions
1145 17th Street, NW
Washington, DC 20036
www.nationalgeographic.com/seas

Sustainable Seas Expeditions
735 State Street
Suite 305
Santa Barbara, CA 93101
www.nationalgeographic.com/seas

Center for Marine Conservation
1725 DeSales Street
Washington, DC 20036
www.cmc-ocean.org

Sea Web
1731 Connecticut Avenue, NW
Washington, DC 10009
www.seaweb.org

National Marine Sanctuary
Program
NOAA
1305 East-West Highway
Silver Spring, MD 20910
www.sanctuaries.noaa.gov

Marine Technology Society
1828 L Street, NW
Washington, DC 20036
www.cms.udel.edu/mts/

National Undersea Research
Program
1315 East-West Highway
Silver Spring, MD 20910
www.noaa.gov
www.uncwil.edu/nurc/

The Explorers Club
46 East 70th Street
New York, NY 10021
www.explorers.org

Illustration Credits
pp. 6, 16, 21, 32, and 44 Al
Giddings; p. 15 Elizabeth R.
Taylor; pp. 26, 29, and 59 Joan H.
Membery; p. 34 Bates Littlehales;
pp. 35 and 37 Flip Schulke; p. 41
Courtesy Steven Miller, NOAA;
pp. 12–13 (art) Francis J. Krasyk;
pp. 60–61 (art) Mark Seidler.
All other illustrations by
Sylvia A. Earle.

INDEX

Illustrations are indicated in **boldface.** If illustrations are included within a page span, the entire span is **boldface.**

The world's largest nonprofit scientific and educational organization, the National Geographic Society was founded in 1888 "for the increase and diffusion of geographic knowledge." Fulfilling this mission, the Society educates and inspires millions every day through magazines, books, television programs, videos, maps and atlases, research grants, the National Geography Bee, teacher workshops, and innovative classroom materials. The Society is supported through membership dues and income from the sale of its educational products. Call 1-800-NGS-LINE for more information. Visit our Web site: www.nationalgeographic.com

$16.11   9/2001

SUNSET ELEMENTARY SCHOOL

627 EAR

28287

Dive! : my adventures in the